D.E. Novak

Eugene and Me

TALES OF ORDINARY WEIRDNESS

ISBN: 978-1-955026-51-2

Published by Ballast Books
www.ballastbooks.com

This is dedicated to Toki and Puff who consistently kept me company along this ride. And for the ones who believed in me: Aaron Blake, Brett Firestone, The Cougars (Al, Cass, and Dani), Matthew Smith, Maureen Cullen, Ray Nelson, and Reed and Julie Lucas. You all have my undying appreciation and love. This would not have been possible without you.

And to all the people of Eugene, Oregon,
thank you for resurrecting my muse.

Chapter 1

WHAT? WHERE??

"You're moving where?"

"Eugene, Oregon."

"Where??"

"Eugene… Oreg—"

"Why??"

"Because I need a change."

That's how it sounded when I told everyone of the plan. I could have been telling them I was heading to Mars from the looks on their faces.

Eugene where? Eugene who?

Understandably, it's more common for people to set their sights on big cities when they talk of moving—of looking to spread their wings. New York, LA, Chicago, Miami… You know, places folks normally go to grab the brass ring and make their mark. It's the dream, right? Well, it was never really mine.

My story began in central New Jersey, so I was close to that haste from the time I was born until the age of eighteen. I felt I already knew what was living there in the brightly lit, bustling cities because I visited two of the biggest of them often. And they were so much fun to explore and get lost in. However, I knew in my heart a big city was not the place for me indefinitely.

Some back story before moving forward with this little love letter: I grew up between the shadows of the Big Apple and the City of Brotherly Love. Smack dab in the middle of solid Jersey suburbia. Housing developments in Mercer County stretched out for miles, built on what were once cornfields and sod farms. Both New York and Philadelphia were roughly an hour's drive from home, and both offered a myriad of culture and interesting things to see and do.

As a kid, it meant visits to Radio City Music Hall, Yankee Stadium, and The Franklin Institute. As a teenager, it meant slacking at Tower Records in Greenwich Village or going for souvlaki on South Street "where all the hippies meet"! I wouldn't have changed it for anything.

Back then, more than half of my friends' parents did the turnpike shuffle to get to work. Otherwise, they took the NJ Transit trains and buses into the cities or sometimes the ferry. So goes life in the 'burbs. They braved a two-hour commute to travel less than sixty miles, plus tolls. That seemed to be the norm. Some people even claimed to thrive on it. Those Type A personalities who actually enjoy living in a pressure cooker.

College committed me to the Appalachian Mountains and moonshine of West Virginia, where I learned to slow down just a little bit. My first year out there, I experienced some culture shock but ended up settling in quite nicely.

After graduation, the first job offer I got unexpectedly landed me in Asbury Park at the Jersey Shore. So, I packed up my things and got set to return to my home state. I stuck around for a while too.

Two careers, a good marriage, and a not-so-good divorce later, I found myself not only still living the Jersey dream but also back in my hometown. The cheapest rent in the area combined with a fabulous swimming pool was what brought me back to an apartment complex I knew well—very well.

Just around the corner from the elementary and junior high school I attended sat the Wynbrook West Apartments. It consisted of sixteen red brick buildings that had been there since the late '60s. These types of garden-style apartments are a staple in almost every town in New Jersey. They all have the same architecture and floor plans, and they were—and still are—everywhere. The only differentiation between them is whether the buildings were built with white brick or red brick and the unique signage that marks each of the complex entrances.

At Wynbrook, the walls were thin, and my building had a serious millipede problem, but the water was always piping hot and included in the monthly rent. That was the closer since long showers have always been appealing to me. My cats would take care of the millipedes, and if I turned the stereo up loud enough, I didn't have to hear my neighbors fuck and fight and fuck some more. It felt like home, and I stayed for more than four years.

My friend Cass and her family lived at Wynbrook from our youth to the time we graduated high school. Memories of her older brother's keg parties and long nights spent bullshitting over teenage drama and family problems would flood back every time I looked at her old balcony. We were resilient kids, and we grew up fast, reared on MTV, microwave dinners, secondhand smoke, and diet Coke. The late-night soft-core porn on cable showed us the hot moves guaranteed to make your boyfriend or girlfriend swoon. It was a learning experience, a new sort of revolution.

You often hear stories of boys stumbling on their father's collection of girly magazines at an early age, but here is where the script gets flipped. My friend Dani had a *wonderfully* progressive mom who just happened to have a stash of Playgirl magazines tucked away in her bedroom. As hormone-addled females, there was *nothing* more intriguing to us at this time in our lives than guys. So, after school, the four of us eighth graders would gather in Dani's bedroom and look. And then we would look some more. Al, Cass, and I got our first real view of the male anatomy thanks to Dani's fabulous mom. Some things you just can't appreciate enough.

Many of my friends' parents were rarely around. So, of course, we resourceful latchkey kids took advantage of this lack of supervision. And by that, I mean we had parties. In fact, we had some *really awesome parties* in their absence. I had one friend who would enter his parents in any and every travel raffle he would come across. This guy successfully won two cruises and a trip to the Grand Canyon for them. Bravo, Chris! You just got yourself three non-consecutive weeks of a parent-free household. Now that is some impressive teenage ingenuity!

Anytime anyone had folks leaving town, it was a giant green flag for a bash, sometimes big, sometimes small, but always happening. If you watch any '80s-era John Hughes movies, you'll get what I mean. I know some of them didn't age well, and many younger generations find these films completely offensive in today's world, but it's really what it was like. Kids took liberties with other kids. A moment here to remind you that we were still learning how NOT to smoke indoors. These were those "teenage dating habits" that were mentioned during the BK Supreme Court nomination hearings. Boys will be boys. And girls will be girls.

During high school, I used to sneak out of thc house on a regular basis and meet up with boys that were just as wound up as I was. Late night encounters fueled by hormones and curiosity. Sometimes it was fun, sometimes it wasn't, and sometimes...

Well, it was a strange time for sure, fresh on the heels of the '60s and '70s sexual revolution when everything turned big: big hair, big makeup, big shoulder pads, and big tits all selling like crazy. Our rock stars wore crotch-hugging hot pants and underwear for outerwear. Would Madonna have been as hot had she not worn lingerie as everyday clothing? It was a sexy time.

I remember listening to Prince's 1999 album in my room one afternoon. My mom came in with some of my laundry, got a good earful, and loudly exclaimed, "It sounds like people are having *SEX* in here!"

I wonder how my grandmother would have reacted if she were in the same circumstance—if it were my thirteen-year-old mother listening to the randy grooves of that record rather than Frank Sinatra or Perry Como. I'm sure Gramma would have blown a fuse. Then again, the women of her generation were good about tolerating domestic violence and a lot of other horrible things, so...

I know it's all relative and that people are products of their environment. Generations of women were subject to all kinds of personal violations that weren't seen as violations at the time. It was just "normal." The cigarettes I used to smoke had a tagline: "You've come a long way, baby!" Yes, we have come a long way. However, we all still have a long, long way to go.

Now, back to the parties! Our senior year of high school, my stepbrother and I had what could only be described as a gathering for the ages. It was supposed to be small.

Noise complaints brought the township cops to the house three times in the course of the evening, and there was a group of gnarly looking dudes from Howard Beach, NY, in my kitchen by night's end. They caught my attention when one of them began guzzling beer out of my mom's two-quart Oster blender pitcher. How this bunch found out about our soiree was anyone's guess. How the cops didn't bust the thing up the first two times around was anyone's guess! Kudos to my stepbrother and his pals for whatever they did there. Perhaps it was that white boy privilege you hear about.

However, the festivities didn't end gently. By dawn, there was a size twelve hole kicked in one of the TV room walls; empty cans, bottles, and cigarette butts were strewn everywhere; and sticky booze stains dotted every fabric surface in the house. It was a disaster, so I guess it's safe to say a good time was had by all.

I thought for sure we'd have our asses handed to us when our parents got back. There was no way in hell we were going to get away with this. But somehow, Joe worked some magic, cleaned up the party mess, and talked us out of that trouble too.

One more time, it was the '80s. The level of parenting for us teenagers was low. *Everyone* was busy working, vacationing, or snorting coke, and those three things were not mutually exclusive. So, we got busy exploring sex and drinking whatever cheap alcohol we could acquire. Again, we grew up fast.

Case in point, by the late '70s, the high school administration got fed up with all the kids smoking cigarettes in the bathrooms, so they delegated a smoking porch located just off the cafeteria. For my oldest sister's Sweet Seventeen party, my parents got a pony keg. I suppose they figured we were going to do these things anyway, so they may as well just give in and supervise—sort of. Generation X, represent!

High school nostalgia aside, there is a quaint feeling to my hometown, a feeling that I will always love, and living there again only reinforced it. I have very fond memories of my childhood growing up during the '70s and am thankful to have been raised in the relative safe haven of the suburbs.

Summers, we picked strawberries at the local turkey farm, and winters, we'd ice skate on the frozen duck pond at the local park or the large patches of water back in the woods behind the neighborhood. We'd walk to the local convenience store and video game arcade to buy candy and drop quarters into the Pac-Man or Space Invaders or Galaga machine. Rebellious teenage me and my equally defiant friends would climb out my bedroom window to smoke cigarettes on the roof.

When autumn rolled around, we would get a good scare out at "Crematory Hill." Before housing developments were built all over Mercer and Monmouth counties, there was a working crematorium tucked back in the woods of Roosevelt Township. The dirt road to get there was littered with no trespassing signs and overgrown with brush, which did absolutely nothing to keep us from going in. Even in the daytime, it was a creepy place, but that's what we were looking for. We wanted to get the shit scared out of us!

The crematory hadn't been operational in a long time, but the gates of the old facility were still standing, off to the side of the road like two stoic iron soldiers guarding the souls of the long departed. The concrete ruins beyond the rusty gates held what looked like and were rumored to be the old ovens, but I never got close enough to verify that. I was too busy peeing my pants and running for the nearest car. Good times!

There were pool parties, sleepovers, barbecues, snowball fights, scavenger hunts, and softball games. Swim meets and dance recitals, snow forts and sledding excursions. Plus, our high school ski club would take a weeklong trip every year. This was not only a way to get a week off of school, but we also received Phys. Ed. credit, so we didn't have to take a gym class for half a semester. It was a win-win.

My sophomore year, we traveled to Mt. Saint Anne, Quebec. Two charter buses filled with kids ages thirteen to seventeen, off in a foreign city with only an 11 p.m. curfew to keep us in check. Yes, we absolutely pushed that boundary. Everyone took advantage of the language barrier and what the city offered us, which were dance clubs and bars for blocks!

By week's end, my sister and one of her friends confidently went out with their ski instructor for drinks. Super cute, blue-eyed, blond-haired Remi picked the two of them up in his little Toyota MR2, and all three zipped off to the nearest tavern. Word travels fast among teenagers, and our "chaperones" did eventually hear about it. The next morning, on the way to the mountain, we all got a lecture on stranger danger. It fell on mostly deaf ears.

Thirteen. That was the magic age when we gained serious independence. Every summer, it was standard for my friends and I to regularly be dropped off at Six Flags Great Adventure for the day. Then, we were left to our own devices until some other parent picked us up at closing time. We were free-range children, usually found in packs of three or six, roaming the park with attitude to spare.

The boys we hung out with would take us on the giant Ferris wheel, and with dumb-ass teenage bravado, they'd take off their shirts, hang out the side of the bucket-like car, and use the shirt to unscrew the searing hot lightbulbs from the wheel. I had a variety of colors displayed on a shelf in my bedroom, a testament to the unbridled foolishness of youth.

We'd also take day trips to Action Park up in Vernon on the fringe of the Pocono Mountains. This place was the amusement park that hit you back! We lovingly referred to it as Traction Park because that's the state you'd end up in at the end of the day at least 50 percent of the time: recovering in traction. Whether it was almost drowning in the wave pool or getting your teeth knocked out inside the infamous cannonball slide, you took your life in your hands with every visit. The scrapes and bruises left behind were badges of honor, and we wore them with pride. Look for the documentary called *Class Action Park*, which showcases just how acutely dangerous that place was. Watch it if you dare.

The much gentler boardwalk and beach town of Seaside Heights was only a forty-minute drive away. You could be there in no time. There, the Casino Pier was another babysitter of sorts with its wealth of rides, a fun house, a haunted house, *and* a freak show.

The Big Top Arcade was where I developed my Skee-Ball addiction. There were so many summers spent barefoot and tan, rolling wooden balls at a bullseye for paper tickets. The smorgasbord of prizes they could be traded for was seemingly endless. The super cool hula girl lamp was what I really coveted. Come Labor Day, I ended up with a plastic happy Hotai Buddha instead, which I thought was just as cool—and even more so after my very Catholic grandmother saw what I had won, then promptly told me to throw it in the ocean, screaming something about graven images and false gods while loudly chastising my mother for raising me wrong. "You need to make sure she goes to mass and CCD, Maureen!"

And that brings us to the garbage memories. There were those, too. Those sneaky little fuckers that resurface when you least expect them to. That cyclical healing process certainly is a harsh bitch, isn't it? I know the memories are just that—memories. I know when they pop up, it's never as severe or as sad a feeling as the real hit was. It's just the dull, achy, tired, old ghosts popping in to say hello. And there were hellos on every corner.

There wasn't a particular occurrence that made me decide to leave my hometown again. It was more like a slow build-up of observations and the realization that things weren't going to change there very much. Almost like a song on repeat. Home was not the place I was meant to be. Home was not good for me anymore. It was time to move on.

But to where? Eugene wasn't my first choice. Truthfully, I barely knew it existed. Portland, sure… But not "the Euge." I contemplated different places: California, Georgia, Colorado, Florida... Nothing seemed appealing. Nothing fit. I ruminated for months. Where is the place for me? Where is it?

Then, on a warm Thanksgiving night at my sister's house, a spark was ignited. My brother-in-law's brother and I were out in the garage after dinner for a post-chow smoke session that was in order on this day of giving thanks and gorging. Brett passed me the joint and said, "Hey, you ever thought about Oregon? I think MG lives there. Maybe you should check it out."

Ding ding ding ding ding! WE HAVE A WINNER!! So, check it, I did.

And I promptly fell in love with Eugene.

Chapter 2

YOU'RE WEIRD

Weird… It's just another word for different. Funky, peculiar, odd, misunderstood even. Here in Oregon, it can be argued that Portland is the city with a lock on weirdness. If that's the only place you see in this state, then sure, it does. However, I beg to differ.

Okay, I know Portland may have oddities like the Unipiper, the Shanghai Tunnels, and the Freakybuttrue Peculiarium. But travel roughly one hundred miles south to TrackTown USA, the land of the Ducks, the Emerald City, and you'll get a real taste of genuine, unfiltered, home-grown weirdness.

Since explorers first started exploring, there have been curious natural sights to observe here in the great outdoors of Oregon. One such spot that boggles the mind and fools the body is simply known as The Vortex. It's described as an area of "naturally occurring visual and perceptual phenomena," which awaits thrill-seeking visitors in the town of Gold Hill. Apparently, gravity loses its force and the laws of physics get a little squirrely down there. You have to experience it to believe it.

There's also the natural wonder of Crater Lake, which is the only dormant volcano lake in the United States. That caldera water is also the deepest and the coldest. Last but not least, we've got Sasquatch!

By Kellis Alexander

By Richard Burr

By Jocelin Fowler –
Maxwell, Plaedo, and Oatmeal

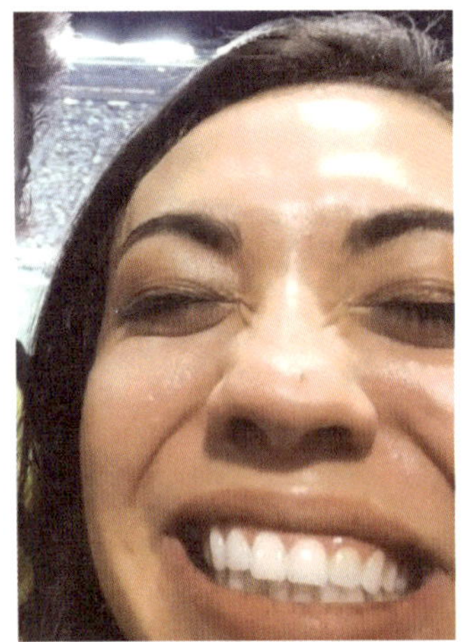

A FEW WEIRDOS

By Richard Burr

By Richard Burr

Before going any further, I feel obligated to get some proper pronunciation across. Most, my former self included, pronounce Eugene YOU-Jean. Emphasis on the "eu." No. Not so. The locals and long-time Oregonians pronounce it yuh-JEAN. Emphasis on the "gene." And just for the record, the proper pronunciation of Oregon is Or-EY-gun. Shall I go on to WillAAAmette? I'll stop for the greater good.

My point with this is that most of this state does things a little differently, and the city of Eugene certainly complies with that unwritten law. A perfect example would be the Mini Pet Mart. This long-established Oregon franchise is a unique combination of pet food and supply/lottery/cigarette store with locations dotting the greater Eugene and surrounding area. Who'd have thought that particular combination would work, but the fact that they are in business and thriving means it does!

Now, back to my love, my emerald. I like to think that the city of Eugene chose me. Like attracts like, birds of a feather, and all that. The weirdness was absolutely palpable when I first visited, and I was smitten from the start—hooked from the first time I broke free of the recirculated airport terminal air and took a deep breath. In the early darkness, it smelled as clean as a newly mown meadow, fresh and flowery. It certainly was a marked improvement from the fart-like stink that usually hits when you get beyond the doors at Newark Liberty. I later saw that there are sheep meadows on both sides of the airport access road. There was all that fresh grass.

The best words to describe this place are "charming" and "earthy." The clouds like to hang in the mountains that border the valley, ancient trees holding them in their piney grip. Everything here is green. The grass never dies in the wintertime, and the moss and lichen grow freely everywhere. And believe me, it does grow EVERYWHERE. It's on concrete highway dividers, on cars, and on wooden light posts as well as all the trees. If you sit still long enough, I'm sure it will grow on you!

Then, the ferns grow out of the moss that grows on the trees. It's life over life over life, an unending cycle. The gigantic Douglas firs live happily alongside yucca and date palms as well as oak and maple trees. Near the corner of Garfield and 8th, there is an enormous prickly pear cactus someone planted long ago that is doing just fine in this temperate climate. The plants here are as varied as the city itself. It is just another sign of the symbiosis and inclusion that permeate the landscape.

That's a BIG cactus

A palm oasis among the firs

Eugene is the second largest city in Oregon. The city itself is chock-full of parks and open space that mercifully has been left undeveloped, and it is surrounded by some of the best scenic riverbank trails for hiking, biking, walking, and, of course, running. Nike was founded here on the same ground Steve Prefontaine, Phil Knight, and Caroline Walker broke records. Describing this place as a sportsman's and outdoorsman's paradise would be an understatement.

The cool green waters of the Willamette and McKenzie rivers converge in our backyard, and these watersheds, combined with the hills on the outskirts of town, host an abundance of wildlife.

Fish and waterfowl are plentiful, but you're also in the territory of cougars, bobcats, and bears. We even had a wild turkey problem a few years ago. They were wandering down into town, making their presence known on Broadway, getting a little too close, freaking out the pedestrians. Gobble, gobble!

By Diane Johnson

The original neighborhoods surrounding the downtown area are mostly 1920s, pastel-painted, craftsman-style homes and ranches. Tree-lined streets, organic neighborhood gardens, and free-range chickens make the scene idyllic. Yes, you can have chickens within city limits! I was thrilled when I saw that. Who else likes eggs?

And who likes aging hippies? Because we've got them as well! Old deadheads, writers, and artists are plentiful here. The Whitaker neighborhood on the north side of town is a haven for them. Brightly painted bungalows glow through the tree-laden, postage-stamp-sized yards, and a kitschy scrap material sculpture sits around every corner. Tibetan prayer flags flutter and sway from front porch awnings. Free artist workshops are a regular occurrence and every Sunday, a community market is set up in Scobert Park and the surrounding streets. The counterculture of the 1960s is still very much alive and well in this small enclave. Sometimes, I think it's because no one ever told them it had passed on elsewhere.

Here in Eugene, we have SLUG Queens. What exactly is a SLUG Queen? Unless you're a local, you probably have no idea. Born out of opposition to a boring and bland city festival name, this annual beauty contest on acid has been a city staple since 1983. SLUG is an acronym for Society of the Legitimization of the Ubiquitous Gastropod. Snails and slugs love it in the Pacific Northwest, those pervasive little fuckers. Like the moss, they are everywhere. However, the SLUG Queen is far from a common creature.

Every August, the pageant holds true to a traditional Miss America contest with three parts: costume, talent, and social question so we can know how quick-witted each contestant is. The queen can be anyone as long as they are over eighteen. Outlandishness is the key to the show, and mockery (both of self and others) reigns. Bribing the judges is expected, and whoever ends up being crowned acts as a goodwill ambassador to the city, showing up at various local functions and fundraising events throughout the year. What a beautiful spot of color for us.

Over near the train station, someone started a shoe tree. It began as a handful of old sneakers and hiking boots hung on a metal ring attached to a maple tree that slowly turned into a multi-tiered chandelier of stilettos, loafers, and sandals. The city said it could stay up for a few months, and people were encouraged to add to it. Group art, outsider art, whatever you want to call it—it is here.

In addition, someone knitted about a dozen duck socks on a prominent railing along Franklin Boulevard. They were green and yellow and had little orange duck feet hanging off their bottoms. Those stuck around for at least six months.

Murals are everywhere; anything and everything can be art—even the bus stops. They all have unique metal work adorning the railings, and there is poetry embossed on the junction boxes. No writer is credited for the works. Only the initials CH are posted:

Trash Panda!

By Diane Johnson

"During the journey from here to there you can travel a thousand places. Places you invent without effort. Places not found on maps or seen in dreams. As your thoughts float through and beyond the world you step into when you arrive."

"It didn't take much to sustain her. She could thrive on trombone music, any song about a song, stardust. As the bandwagon came back around she made up grooves of a tender tune. Only slightly lonely, she opened every window for her blues."

"As we talked a light breeze touched my cheek and colors striped the sky. Even after I woke, what you said continued to sooth me though I didn't remember a single one of your words any better than I could catch a sparrow with my bare hands."

"The jay began to brag for it was nearly summer and a thousand cherries were percolating, gaining one drop of sweetness at a time. They hung way above our reach but the bragging bird could feast and boast all at once, free as a sunbeam."

This is a nice touch! At every stop, there are different stamped and punched metal nature scenes of various flowers and woodland critters, which greet the riders as they head off to take care of their daily business. My favorite is the one I refer to as the Trash Panda stop. The scene is of a raccoon nudging the lid off of a garbage can and an opossum looking on from the wings, hopeful for a snack. This is urban wildlife at its best. It's simply adorable.

The people who reside here in Eugene seem to genuinely love it. "Just another beautiful day in paradise" is what my neighbor often says when we see each other. I can feel the authenticity and kindness that reverberates here.

For instance, this city is extraordinarily handicapped accessible as well as highly LGBT friendly. Not that the two are mutually exclusive; it's just that these two parts of the community are absolutely seen and represented here. There are hundreds of wheelchairs and scooters moving around this town on a daily basis, many of them decorated with pride stickers and flags. To me, that's just two underdogs rolling on into one!

By Diane Johnson

By Diane Johnson

The gold medal for creativity goes to the couple seen cruising single file up an Echo Hollow Road bike lane on their motorized jazzy scooters. These rides were tricked out, adorned with all sorts of colored flags, with stuffed animals secured in the framework of the vehicle. In the front basket of the woman's ride sat a tiny Yorkie dog, calm as a Hindu cow, taking it all in, ears flapping in the wind, tongue hanging awkwardly from its mouth. What a life.

And then, there are the bicycles. Oh, *SO* many bicycles here. This is a city that asks, "Why drive a car when you can ride a bike?!" Plastic bubble bike covers exist so you can ride in the bona fide Pacific Northwest rain! Did you know that? The first time I saw one of these contraptions, I about died. Actually, the guy on the bike was the one who about died because I almost ran over him! In my defense, it was dark, and I was still new in town. But who the hell rides around like that? Eugenians, that's who! Bottom line though—everyone is rolling. As long as you don't roll over someone's foot, their kid, or their pet, you're golden.

"Friendly" is another fitting adjective for Eugene. Everyone here is friendly. Dolly Parton even wrote a song about us and how her homesick heart was soothed by the graciousness of this place: "Eugene, Oregon, you were kind, the love you gave was genuine. You gave me inspiration and the strength to carry on. And I won't be forgetting all the kindness that you showed to a homesick country girl a long, long way from Tennessee." You're so on it, Dolly! But I change the lyrics to "a not-so-homesick girl a long, long way from New Jersey" when I sing it.

Hands down, it's one of the friendliest cities around. There's even a neighborhood here known as The Friendly, and Friendly Street runs through it. See a pattern here?

Going along with the communal tendencies of this place, a good number of restaurants and brew pubs in town are outfitted with big and long tables that everyone just shares. Think Oktoberfest beer garden, and you're in the right ballpark. If there's room, just pull up a bench and join the folks already there. It's a sharing community.

Little libraries are a staple as well as tiny food pantries and community vegetable gardens. Take what you need. Give back when you can.

As an example, not too long ago, I spotted a little art gallery. It was just a small, brightly painted box, which held a few tiny three-by-three paintings and a calligraphy scroll. The small canvases were modern in style; Kandinski meets Pollak would be the best description. The scroll looked like a sampler of sorts, the alphabet written out in both upper- and lowercase by an unknown hand.

A few years back, here was even a Eugene resident who would go out to the I-5 exits and simply wave to the passing vehicles just to spread the love. Just to make someone smile. Every day, I am surprised and more impressed.

Yes, it's a happy city. Yes, it's an inclusive city, but no place is a perfect utopia. I absolutely know there are a handful of jerks squirreled away somewhere in the hills of this town, but I also know the majority of the population comprises super laidback individuals. All in all, I know the asshole quotient in my life dropped significantly once I moved here compared to my east coast experiences.

Honestly, there have only been two stand-out times I witnessed displays of jackassery. One was at a pharmacy, and the fellow was ranting about his migraine medicine, but I guess he gets a pass since no one likes a migraine. The other was this older man at a local brew pub. I was saving two seats for friends, and this septuagenarian just came up and started dragging away the bar stools.

"Hey, those are being saved!" I said to him.

He looked at me with a stinky side-eye and mumbled something about women showing respect.

My buddy Zac then chimed in with, "Well, respect goes both ways, sir."

Guess who got the stink eye then? Pops didn't like our sass—not one bit. I'm not certain, but I think he may have been wearing a MAGA hat. Either way, he seemed entitled. But that's it. That's all I've experienced as far as bad behavior goes. And I like that low number.

People don't complain about much in this city, but when they do, the three biggest issues seem to be the influx of homeless individuals, the influx of Californians, and traffic. They complain, but they don't know what bad traffic really is. I think they'd implode if they encountered a true LA- or NY-style backup.

Or maybe they'd just sit quietly and wait in the righthand lane. See, Eugene road rage can best be described as three cars coming to a four-way stop. Then, the politeness dance begins... You first. No, YOU first. Noo, YOU first... It's madness. Someone PLEASE make a decision and stick to it!

As a way to advise the public on correct driving maneuvers, the Department of Transportation recently issued a press release and erected huge highway signs, instructing our kind citizens to "merge like a zipper" when dealing with road work and lane closures. That's because native Eugenians think it's rude to cut in line and will stay at a dead stop rather than use an open lane.

Eugene is a city, but it's the first one I've lived in where no one knows how to parallel park. If you see someone doing it correctly, they are not from here! Give Eugenians a space as big as a semi-trailer, and they still can't do it. I've watched and laughed, then yelled, "CUT THE WHEEL BACK," as they stared like deer in headlights. I don't know what it is, and I can't explain it—it just is.

One time, amazement ensued when a guy stopped *right in the middle of his turn* into a strip mall parking lot because he'd seen a friend pulling out and wanted to talk to him. I watched in bewilderment as two cars slowly rolled up, then stopped behind this yutz. Then, a third… Then, a fourth… No one honked. No one yelled. I just sat and watched while waiting for my light to turn green. Back east, the expletives would be flying over a symphony of horns. I just sat in awe at the calm.

Honestly, no one is in a hot rush for anything in this town. Maybe it's the weed. Okay, it's probably the weed. Comparatively speaking, I'd put the pace here in the same league as Georgia or the Carolinas. Let's meander, let's saunter, let's enjoy this beautiful day. It's only one of the reasons why I'm here.

Living in Eugene has absolutely taught me patience and acceptance, and that is a very good thing. It has cemented the fact that not everyone is alike or abled, and I truly needed that lesson.

There was a time when I would have been fuming if I'd gotten stuck waiting for more than two minutes in line at a store. Like at the dispensary, waiting behind some hairy farmer dude who's passionately commiserating his horrible weed grow situation to the budtender… My blood pressure would be slowly rising, my jaw slowly clenching. Now, I simply think, *What's another minute or two? Just step back and observe the exchange.*

Sometimes, you'll hear interesting or informative or funny stuff. I've lost count of how many clerks and checkout people have asked, "Any plans for the day/weekend?" while I'm bagging up my groceries or beer or pot. That is the norm here. They all do it. It's nice, I guess. Regardless, it is a part of this environment, and I know that behavior is not going anywhere. Now, when they ask, sometimes I'll make up my own weird stories on the fly. It can be amusing. Just as long as no one is waiting behind me.

Chapter 3

THE SIGHTS (YOU'RE WEIRD PART 2)

When you come to Eugene, you will see plenty of interesting and sometimes inexplicable things. Things you probably never thought you'd see. Honestly, I'm sure this place is why the phrase "truth is stranger than fiction" was coined. This is a town spilling over with free expression.

One of the first bits of weirdness I witnessed was a guy in a Ronald Reagan mask mowing his lawn. Now, that's something you don't see every day. I howled with laughter at this bizarre scene! Was this some sort of social commentary? Was this performance art? I will never know. Shortly after that came the person wearing a cow costume, complete with pink udders, walking their dog in a rainstorm. They had a SpongeBob umbrella, which completed the look.

Costumes are normal here. It's not uncommon to see people wearing fairy or angel wings while shopping or riding local transit. Beer costumes have been plentiful lately. Have you seen a beer drinking a beer? Beer cannibalism!

Just last week, there was a pack of Teletubbies on the south end of town, waddling toward who knows what sort of antics. And my friends Jon and Taylor have been known on occasion to go drinking downtown in their bacon costumes. It's a conversation starter, for sure.

By Jonathan Garth

Then, there's the King who hangs out on Oak St. I've seen him several times, draped in a royal blue velvet robe and wearing a crown proclaiming him "#1" in rainbow glitter. He was a noble sight, strutting his stuff on the sidewalk. Your highness, rock on! Fly that freak flag proudly.

Here, there are angels at the supermarket and pirates at the ice rink. One afternoon, I spied a young lad sporting a badass '80s-style rat tail hairdo walking his pet box turtle up at Skinner Butte Park. He said every pet deserves a walk in the fresh air. I agree.

Another time, I spied a Star Wars stormtrooper riding shotgun in a Toyota. The driver was a regular dude. It was a few days before May the 4th, so perhaps the stormtrooper was giving his costume a dry run before the actual "holiday." It's also possible this fellow was just feeling like a stormtrooper that day. In Eugene, you never really know.

I'm always wondering when I'll see the next bit of visual fun and what exactly it will be this time. For instance, I once spied a woman wearing what looked like a genuine space suit helmet. Like from NASA. She was just ambling down 11th Ave., wearing a sundress and a hat built for outer space. There's nothing odd about that, right? The other day, it was a guy walking his pig—his big, 200-pound pig—in a pink harness.

On the automotive end, there's a Jeep in town with a full-size skeleton dressed up in a life vest and old-time pilot goggles. He's wedged between the back of the vehicle and its spare tire. Femurs and fibulas and tibias dangle out below, free and easy, blowing in the wind. Before you assume that it may have been a Halloween decoration, I should mention it was July when I first observed this. Last March, I saw "Skelly" cruising on the west side, sporting a fuzzy, green top hat, clearly preparing for St. Patrick's Day.

Modern covered wagon

One last fine ride I can't leave out is the baby blue VW Bug adorned with various doll heads. They are mostly Barbie heads, glued on in a Mohawk-type pattern from the front to the rear bumper. There are also some odd-sized, beat-up straggler heads attached to the car doors and running boards, making it look more chaotic than it already is. This is such an interesting place.

Another notable fixture in Eugene is the renowned outdoor Saturday Market, which runs half the year from April to October. It's a lively few blocks filled with artisans selling locally produced clothing, jewelry, hats, leather goods, paintings, puzzles, games, rocks, crystals, and countless other items you never knew you needed. It's a feast for the senses when the local food trucks fire up their grills and offer a sumptuous variety of Thai, Ethiopian, Jamaican, and Indian delicacies for your hungry belly. Plus, there is always a changing lineup of talented local musicians gracing the market public stage for your listening enjoyment throughout the day. The farmers' market is there as well, overflowing with all kinds of organic produce, fresh flowers, spices, and local honey.

Across the street from the market, in front of the county courthouse ironically, is what I refer to as the Smoking Section. In this area dwells a slightly grittier tribe. There's almost always a drum circle in progress, and the scent of incense hangs heavy in the air. Rouge weed dealers scout the area for underage kids so they can sell their two-dollar grams. This is also where you can get hand-carved hash pipes, dream catchers, and all types of metaphysical utensils.

I've seen plenty of unique bumper stickers around town, and Saturday Market is always the best place to find them:

I brake for butterflies.
Kiss me, I'm organic.
I heart unicorns.
I'm pro-Sasquatch and I vote!
Cow hugger
Tree Cheers for the Arboretum!
There's no place like Om.
No Mediocre!
White Lies Matter
Live a Great Story
Rural, not stupid: Biden 2020.
These are just a few of the highlights.

The one sticker that made me laugh out loud with a true, heart-felt guffaw was the one I spied on the back of an enormous F350 pickup truck. *Size Matters*. That's all it said. Okay, I know country boys like to brag on their rides, but the beautiful part was when I saw the driver get out of the cab. This fellow couldn't have been taller than a ten-year-old. Seriously, he was five feet at best. Oh dear. Oh my. Someone has issues. Isn't it ironic? Don't you think? Yeah, I really do think.

To counteract those types of ridiculous encounters, in Eugene, there are often big, sturdy men wearing sparkly sequined skirts and flowing island sarongs. They wear skirts of all kinds actually, most likely purchased at one of the many St. Vinnie's or Goodwill thrift stores here in town. There are plenty of kilts too. I say if you have nice legs, you may as well show them off, right?

Like the Record Guy. I first saw this character at the local Picc-A-Dilly Flea Market, where he had a table selling old record albums. You can't help but notice his presence when you walk into the building. And boy, what a presence! An extremely tall fellow with gaunt features and long, black hair, he looks like a cross between the musicians Marilyn Manson and Joey Ramone. Marilyn Ramone, if you will. I see him biking around town on a regular basis, usually dressed up with a colorful tutu over his black spiderweb tights, his long legs pumping, jetting him and his Schwinn through the streets, off to procure more vintage vinyl to flip at the flea.

Another local favorite on a bicycle is the U of O Jesus Guy. He is a senior gentleman whose bike and attached cart are covered in plastic dollar store flowers and University of Oregon flags. He has hanging signs that read "I heart Eugene, OR," "Go Ducks," and "God loves U Trust Jesus." He's fused his love of the U with his love for Jesus and will spread the word to everyone. One more shining example of a person doing their own thing in a place that utterly thrives on it.

You simply never know what you will run across. Here in Eugene, all of that daily expressive artistic absurdity is the norm, and that's the most beautiful thing about it. Face the day with humor, don't hurt anyone, and do what makes you happy.

One of the grooviest senior citizens on planet Earth does just that. I used to see her playing her electric guitar downtown in Kesey Square, sharing her amazing shredding abilities with the other buskers. A petite Asian woman in camouflage pants and turquoise blue hair, she is a total punk rock throwback. The first time I saw her, it was clear this lady had better things to do than play bingo or pickleball in her golden years. Stargazer is what she's known by, and she now occasionally performs on the corner of 18th and Oak Patch, wailing on her Stratocaster like a boss, playing to the heavens or to anyone else who'll listen.

As you may recall, I spoke of everyone rolling in this town. If that isn't true, I don't know what is. See above re: Marilyn Ramone and the Jesus Guy. Bikes and power chairs are plentiful, but so are skateboards and scooters, both motorized and those little kick types.

I've witnessed a girl riding on her longboard, playing acoustic guitar while coasting down a 20 percent grade in the bike lane. That was impressive! There was another kid on a skateboard that got my attention. This one was holding three large trout on a giant hook while he cruised down 6th Street, his friend right behind him, fishless. To me, it resembled a modern version of Tom Sawyer and Huck Finn, and it made me smile.

Additionally, I've gleefully observed plenty of dogs on skateboards here. More than I can count, actually. And, yes, some of those pups were wearing hats while rolling. How can you not grin at any animal wearing a hat? I don't think it can be done.

I once spied a man on an old Harley motorcycle, and in the bike's sidecar sat a gigantic, drooling Rottweiler adorned with a trapper hat. He looked happy as a clam, secure in the knowledge that he rocked that hat better than Elmer Fudd could any day.

Standard poodles with the silly haircut always look goofy to me, but here in Eugene, there is one whose owner bumped it to the next level by dying its head and ankle puffs pink—bright, shocking Pepto Bismol pink. I must admit, that bitch had style.

Other critters are not exempt from the weirdness here. A young lady walking down Franklin Avenue caught my eye one day. It looked like she was wearing a tall, Lincoln-like top hat from afar, but the closer I got, I realized the hat was really a black cat balanced perfectly on top of her head. Color me impressed.

And a simple trip to the gas station truly made my afternoon when I noticed the truck in front of me. The driver was an older man, probably in his 70s, wearing what looked like a pool dress and those old-school jelly sandals. He looked ready for summer in his breezy and bright outfit. His wife sported a tattered Jack Daniel's T-shirt, cut-off shorts, and a small parrot on her shoulder. Birdy was enjoying himself by flying back and forth from Mr. Pool Dress's arm to Ms. Cut-Offs' head, whistling and chirping away while they filled the tank. They were a fun sight. A happy little family with zero fucks to give. Bless this place.

The shoeless punk rock girl I saw talking to a naked baby doll she was holding was another WTF moment, but not in a good way. That observation most certainly did not make me smile. There are many that are shoeless here. Mental health and the homeless crisis remain a big problem. Eugene is a community of caring and has a reputation for being a gentle place, which is why they come. We have services available.

Here, the homeless are referred to as the unhoused. These are the urban campers who make the sidewalks and green areas of the city their home. As a way to combat this, the local housing authority approved for small Conestoga Huts to be built for what is now known as the city's Safe Sleep Sites. Eugene also approved the creation of new micro areas and pallet shelters. The demand for more has been steadily growing. These plots offer people showers, laundry facilities, and one meal a day. R/V and trailer parking is available as well.

Scattered throughout the city, some of these sites are fenced outdoor areas, and some have been constructed in unused warehouse space rented out by the city. There are solar panels on the roofs at a few of these areas . The effort is absolutely inspiring, and these tiny communities have become a place of hope for many—so many that there is a waitlist for services.

But sometimes, help comes too late. Sometimes, they die on the streets. Roughly 30 percent of the homeless do not want help. Many feel they are sovereign citizens—that just by being an American, they have the right to make use of any public lands. They feel so strongly about this that they refuse any help, even when the weather turns bad.

Several years ago, there was a local news report of a dead man found in a dumpster behind a downtown Jiffy Lube. My friend Addie said he was probably a homeless guy who'd climbed in trying to keep warm and then died from exposure. Being from Jersey, this was off to me. If you find a body in a dumpster, someone most likely put it there!

But I digress. Our city's low-cost medical White Bird Clinic and their Crisis Assistance Helping Out on the Streets (CAHOOTS) team are changing the way domestic disputes and other non-life-threatening situations are being handled. In fact, their playbook is now being used as a model for other cities to follow. The clinic team was even a spotlight feature on NBC Nightly news in 2020.

Their trick is simple: They send in counselors rather than cops to de-escalate potentially dangerous situations. No guns, no flashing lights or sirens, just someone to talk it out with. I'm happy to report that CAHOOTS has had an overwhelmingly positive outcome with this system, and it only continues to improve lives and help those who need it most. People and lives have always been complex. The only thing that changes is how we deal with and help them.

But what to do with the ones who don't want help? That's the real test. Some are so deep in the throes of mental illness that they don't realize how dangerous their situation really is.

For example, the guy who dresses like a renegade pirate and camps out on the corner of 18th and Chambers certainly doesn't seem to want help. Would Jack Sparrow want help? Probably not, regardless of the severity of his situation or mental state.

Several months back, I did notice what looked like one of his pirate boots laying lonely on the sidewalk where he camped. It sat there like a sad, makeshift testament to the swashbuckler whose ill head may not have even registered it was missing in the first place. Perhaps he was trying for an authentic peg leg. Or maybe he did have a moment of clarity and chose to take some offered help. I'll never know. And when you don't know, all you can do is hope the seas carry them safely until they reach their journey's end.

Chapter 4

SMALL BUSINESSES, SMALL NEIGHBORHOODS, BIG FUN

Local business is not immune to the oddness of this place. Yes, of course, we have the big-box stores out on the edges of town and at the mall, but we truly have some incredible small businesses here in Eugene.

Let's start with Hirons, the town's oldest pharmacy/five-and-dime store. When you step inside this institution, you are greeted by a swirling, colorful vortex of nostalgia. I've heard newbies audibly gasp and blurt out "WHOA" when they walk through the door. Chinese paper lanterns hang above the aisles. Spinning animal mask displays and feather boas float in the incense-scented artificial breeze. Wind chimes tinkle over the piñatas, and plastic Hawaiian leis share shelf space with Christmas lights. It's the place to get all football gameday supplies, including flasks, rain gear, and grills. You can also fill a prescription, mail a letter, and buy a birthday card. It is old-school, one-stop shopping at its finest. A true gem with two convenient locations!

Where the technicolor party accessories grow

You know you want a plush duck!

More stuff you never knew you needed

I'm a sucker for smart and witty advertising—I always have been—and the television advertising for local businesses here is just that: unique, funny, and absolutely deserving of all kinds of recognition. Most local advertising outside of big city markets has a tendency to be campy and/or low budget. Not here. And in the creativity department, Jerry's Home Improvement holds the title for best commercials ever.

Jerry's is the local competition to the big home improvement stores, and their spots consistently crack me up. In all of them, it looks like they're using standard stock footage of people doing home improvement things or just home-type stuff like having a BBQ or dance lessons in the living room. But the voiceover track doesn't quite match up with the actor's lips. Think old-school kung-fu movies or any English-dubbed foreign film from the '60s. It's goofy and fun and endearing, and I adore it.

They also do some pretty cute spots with dogs. However, their current animal feature is emperor penguins slipping and sliding all over the place and taking headers into the water. "Better head for Jerry's to stock up on winter supplies!"

Then, there is Midgleys Stove & Fireplace Center. Their ads prominently feature who I refer to as Mr. Midgley or, lovingly, The Midge. He looks like a cross between Sam Elliott and George Clooney, and he'll tell you all about the perks of having Midgleys come out and service your fireplace before the weather gets cold. Sometimes, he picks up his acoustic guitar and sings the pitch to you, ending with their tagline, "Go anywhere else and you're just playing with fire."

The Midge

Ugggghhh… I'm smitten. But I was much more than that when I met him in person. I was working part time as a temperature checker in the front lobby of one of the local hospitals during the pandemic, and he came walking in to visit with his brother. Everyone was masked up, so I couldn't see much of his face, but when he spoke… *That voice. I know that voice!*

"You're Mr. Midgley!" I shouted like some giddy idiot schoolgirl.

"A-yuh… I am," he responded.

Between dopey giggles, I shared that my girlfriends and I all love his commercials. He gave me a wink and told me not to play with fire. Oh yes, I'm now officially in love.

And finally, there is Ask the Bug Man, which is a pest removal company that went old school with its advertising. They used 1950s stock footage of the movie *The Wolfman* with a voice-over complaining about having fleas. He's howling "I've got fleeeeeeas! What should I dooooooooo?" And the witch—well, she has moles. She's asking the mirror, mirror on the wall about them. Mirror tells her to see a dermatologist. She vehemently responds, "Not on my face—in my yard!" Then, *The Giant Spider Invasion* footage rolls out every spring. "You'd better be ready for them!" is the voiceover heard while grainy images of fifty-foot-tall spiders wreak havoc on us humans.

I'd honestly like to give these companies my own award for creative achievement in the field of advertising if they haven't gotten some accolades already.

The creativity flows over into our local music scene, which is eclectic and impressive—so much so that it rivals some of the biggest cities on the west coast. From the classical performances of the Eugene Symphony to the grittiest rap, you can find it here.

For instance, the Satin Love Orchestra, the true musical veterans of this city, have been bringing their funky disco hits to the masses with flair to spare since 1997. And there is Fortune's Folly, who I would describe as an energetic alternative rock power trio with an absolute firecracker for a frontwoman. The energy that emanates when they play is nothing short of intoxicating.

Oh, sweet mother of punker, do you like to mosh? If so, then Pirate Radio is the band for you. Their smart and original tunes take me back to a time when that genre ruled my cassette deck. Oi! We've also got musical dynamo Plaedo, who recently released "Empires Die…Life Evolves," one of the most epic rap albums I've listened to in a long time. And I can't forget the ever-diverse Maxwell Davis! When I play his music, it holds its own against heavy hitters like Eminem and Alt-J. All of these fantastic and dedicated artists can be found and supported on Spotify as well as the usual social media platforms.

Oh yeah, and there's the Hult Center for the Performing Arts, the Cuthbert Amphitheater, and the McDonald Theatre, which all attract headlining musical acts from around the world. There is rarely a lack of good concerts here. Catching a touring production of the latest hit musical at the Hult rivals Broadway—and at half the price!

And if *you* happen to be the dramatic sort and want to hit the stage and flex your acting chops, you can get involved with the Very Little Theatre also known as the VLT. Located on Hilyard Street, it's one of the longest-running and most successful community theatres in the country. They've been doing comedy, drama, and musicals there since 1929 and have no plans to stop.

Here in Eugene, outsider art is abundant throughout the neighborhoods, and creativity flourishes everywhere. There are plastic chickens on rooftops and decoy geese on telephone poles. (Speaking of geese, the live ones are a little weird too in that I've seen them land and sit on rooftops). There are little stone castles standing sturdy in side yards and bedroom windows taped up with cut-out pictures of eyes or lips or hands. You'll see decorated junction boxes and water meters painted up like skulls with glowing red eyes as well as awesome privacy fences made from old painted doors.

This goose is fake.
Who put it up there?

These geese are real.
Do they normally land on rooftops?

Imposter #2

By Diane Johnson –
Johnny's got his eye on you!

By Diane Johnson

I hope this never goes away.

When I first arrived, I noticed an apartment complex on Willamette St. that had a tapestry of Nicholas Cage's face flying from a second-floor balcony. This epic drapery hung there for more than five years. It disappeared recently for about six months, to my dismay, but then made a stellar comeback. The tenants had hung up not one but TWO Nics! Maybe in another year, there will be three.

Let me tell you how the '80s version of me totally wanted to high-five the kids who lived in the house near campus off Olive St. They had an old-school magazine photo cut-out of John Stamos in his prime adorning their front door window. His hair was magnificent.

John is gone from that window now, but that's the thing about this place. Something else equally amusing will show up sooner or later. It's gospel. Fixtures in this town do eventually go away, and in their place, a new peculiarity is born. Every day, there is something novel to see here. It's the quirky circle of life.

Humor and whimsy aside, Eugenites do care about important things: social things, environmental things, things that many other people just let pass simply due to circumstances that encompass a busy life. There are protests and marches, support groups and communal gatherings. And the *Eugene Weekly*, our free city paper, is there to cover it all and distribute it to the public. The sense of community here is to be admired, especially when every voice, even the smallest, is encouraged to speak. However you choose to express yourself, it's welcomed.

And many here will get on their soap box, especially if they feel strongly enough. I inadvertently listened to a woman while waiting in line at the pharmacy. It was at the height of the pandemic, and she was talking with the pharmacist about recent COVID restrictions. She mentioned how Anne Frank's family toughed it out together in an attic for two years. "The least we can do is stay home," she said. *Oh dear, sweet lady... If only we had more of your way of thinking in the world. Please keep saying these things out loud so everyone can hear.*

One of my favorite homes in Eugene is the one I call the Temple House. It sits at the corner of 18th and City View and has an impressive presence. It's a brightly painted ranch-style duplex, yellow with red trim, but that's not what will grab your attention. Off to the left side of the curved drive sits a twenty-foot concrete statue of Buddha, seated calmly, awaiting prayers. He's surrounded by a multitude of other smaller Buddhas, foo dogs, pagodas, and garden planters. Paper lanterns hang from the rain gutters. The house is beautifully maintained, and rose gardens flank the property line.

Above the front door, there are dual flag poles, one flying the flag of the Republic of China (1912 – 1949) and one with the U.S. flag. When I drove past one day during our 45th president's administration, Old Glory was flying upside down. Yes, indeed, my friend, we are most certainly in distress. Freedom of expression once again making its mark in a town that was made for it.

Last but not least, perhaps the most unique building in Eugene is the Shelton McMurphey Johnson House or, as it's fondly called, the castle on the hill. There's a certain Addams Family vibe to it at first glance—probably at second glance too. A large Queen Anne-style home, it sits up on the Skinner Butte hillside, overlooking the whole town. The muted greens and blues of the paint scheme blend in with the trees, making it seem almost one with the forest that grows up the hill behind the property.

The mansion on the hill

It is used as a historical museum mostly, but the house can be rented for parties. Throughout the year, the management arranges all sorts of neat events and afternoon tea socials, which are open to the public. The summer of 2022, they hosted a Victorian finishing school. Now I wonder who couldn't use some proper manners in this day and age. Everyone should know it is always right to keep your pinkie extended while sipping your Kombucha!

My favorite street artist's early work.

Her evolution.

Chapter 5

TRAVEL

Two thousand nine hundred miles was the distance I had to drive to get here. It would be an adventure, one that I was excited about and so absolutely ready for. So, I got a tow hitch put on the Mazda and started planning the move. I knew getting out here would mean travel—a lot of it—by both air and car.

When I first visited, I stayed with Michael. We had gone to high school together, but after reconnecting at our twenty-year reunion, we had formed more of a friendship on Facebook. His home was an old, rustic, two-story contemporary nestled in the south hills. Enormous fir trees ringed the backyard, and deer would come by and feed on the blackberry bushes. Wild turkeys often picked and scratched through the tall grass that led into the woods. It was lovely.

He took me out to the coast one afternoon to show me how easy it is to escape into nature from the city when you need to. Through Florence and up to Cape Perpetua, we drove through the forests of the Cascade coastal range mountains and ended up on a seaside cliff. The clouds hang in the mountains out here too, and they blow up the rugged hills and envelop you.

As we stood looking out at the roiling Pacific, one of those clouds rolled in. My lungs felt cold and shivery as I breathed in the icy vapor. It was primal. I was one with the cumulonimbus cloud. At that moment, I knew I needed to move here and that it was going to be amazing once I did. Any doubt I'd previously had on the matter simply furled away with my exhale and those clouds.

And now, let's get back to reality from my dreamy, mist-filed state. I adore traveling. For the most part, I always have. The excitement of jetting off to a new location has always made me happy. I also believe road trips should be taken often and started at the youngest age possible.

I had been through the Pacific Northwest before as a kid when my paternal grandparents took me and my cousin Jason on a winding cross country road trip from Arizona to New Jersey. It was the summer of 1981. Great-uncle Johnny's relatives lived somewhere outside of Portland, so we made it a stop along the journey. I have vivid memories of my grandfather taking us up to Mt. Saint Helens, which had blown up just the year before. Climbing the ash-covered hillside in his sturdy yellow 1975 Oldsmobile V8 sedan, he drove around several roadblocks so we could get a better look at the destruction, my grandmother screaming and yelling at him to turn around the entire time.

On that note, there seems to be a lack of delight in most travelers these days. There's not enough of that "enjoy the ride" mentality, but I get it. It's hurried most of the time, and if you are traveling with a group, it can make things even more trying. There are crowds, delays, and rude people. But there's also a tremendous amount of hilarity. And during the back and forth of relocating, I observed it everywhere.

The first cab I hailed here in Eugene is a fine example. As I hoisted my bag into the trunk, my very Polish-sounding cab driver said loudly, "STRONG GIRL! FARM?" Going forward, I will introduce myself as such.

As we all know, to make the time pass a little more quickly in airports and on flights, at least half the people you encounter while traveling will want to talk, of course. With anyone who will listen. And even if you seem like you don't want to listen, they're still going to talk.

Let me brief you about the seventy-something-year-old man who sat down across from me in Salt Lake City. He kept going on about how his phone was made in AMERICA! How the ones from "Kor-EEE-uh" are crap. Five minutes into his diatribe, he said he couldn't get a signal and asked if my phone was working. Isn't it ironic? Don't you think?

Then, there was the other oldster on my flight to Denver, wearing his military flyboy hat and matching bomber jacket. As soon as the plane started up, this character started yelling at the top of his lungs, "FIRE ENGINE ONE! FIRE ENGINE TWO!" and so on. He was enjoying himself immensely and didn't care if the whole plane heard it. Reliving his glory days as a pilot, no doubt. Thank you for your service, sir, and for being your awesome self.

In one case, the not-so-fun talkative passenger was a strange lady bound for Seattle. She was either off her meds or perhaps *on* some questionable recreational elixir, talking loudly about her role in weaponizing Google for the government and other crazy tech stuff. Any time anyone mentions weaponizing anything, I'm out. I felt really bad for her seatmate.

She would have been a perfect candidate to share a row with the guy talking about how his son covertly removed, then dismantled, a supercomputer from Area 51. That was one of the more interesting conversations I had the pleasure of overhearing. I wanted to jump in and ask if there was evidence of alien life found but decided against it when he started picking his nose. He clapped when we landed.

At SFO, it was the obnoxious businessman sitting behind me, shouting into his phone about money and stocks and bottom lines. This was teamed up with his five-year-old, who started screaming for reasons unknown, maybe to try to emulate Daddy. Mom stepped in to try to calm the situation with "Hey, buuuuuddy… What's going on? Colton??" (Or Bronson, or maybe it was Jagger.) "Wanna take a selfie?" With that, the kid started screaming even louder. "NOOOOOOOOOOOOOOOOOOOO!" Looked like this family vacation was off to a roaring start.

As I've observed, at least half the people in airports or any random station have their face buried in a device or phone. It's who we are as a society, and I do my best to adapt to it. I do enjoy seeing other people like me though—the ones who look around. There aren't many of us, so when I do come across them, I always give them the thumbs-up.

For example, when I was in the Minneapolis airport on a layover, I had time to kill, so I wandered until I found a java joint. While in line for coffee, a catchy song started playing over the shop's sound system, and the lady beside me began bobbing up and down, feeling the beat. Then, she really started dancing. And I did too! We both just danced in place for a solid two minutes. What fun! When we stopped, she turned toward me, and I noticed she was a pilot for Sun Country. We talked a bit, and she shared that she'd been flying for twenty-six years. Strong girl! Make that strong woman. You just keep on dancing.

The last leg of this journey, actually getting the last of my things out to Eugene, was an adventure I'll never forget. Our crew consisted of my dear buddy George, me, three cats, and a betta fish, all packed tight in my little Mazda. The U-Haul hitched to the back held all my really important stuff that couldn't go in the PACK-RAT container. Both of us laughed at U-Haul's 55 mile an hour "suggested maximum speed" stickers posted on both wheel wells.

By George MacLeod – copilot George and navigator Gretta

The journey across the country took exactly 52.5 hours; we absolutely cannon-balled it, stopping only to refuel, use the bathroom, and pick up mini-mart food and coffee. We did treat ourselves once by stopping at a Shoney's somewhere in Nebraska for an actual meal, but that was it. We were on a mission.

This road trip was the first time I had ever encountered frozen fog, which is like normal fog, but when the headlights catch the frost crystals… Wow! Rainbow halos swirling and looping in front of the car made me feel slightly off balance. It was intense. Once the fog cleared, the moonlight lit up the snow-capped mountains and made visible the arctic hares that sat near the side of the road. Let me tell you, these are some big bunnies! Mostly white with some dark spots and about the size of a small dog. How they survive in negative-twenty-degree temperatures was a reminder of just how resilient and well-equipped nature is and how fragile humans are.

Along the way, I was introduced to the Kum & Go. This is the premier travel/truck stop of the northern states. The name alone wins it. At 3 a.m., we came rolling in, slightly delirious, trying to shake the highway hypnosis. I went looking for the bathrooms only to find an out of order sign. So, I asked the girl at the counter where to go. She said to just go use the showers. I replied, "You want me to pee in the shower?" not realizing that this is a fucking truck stop and they have full-on bathrooms, not just toilets. At that moment, I felt a long way from home and very dumb. George just laughed.

We saw a real cowboy outside the town of Sisters when we stopped for gas. He wore a ten-gallon hat, cowhide chaps, and a handlebar mustache that any hipster would envy. His horse was parked outside, and I swear that filly looked at us and thought, "Good luck, city folk" as we sloppily skidded and slid while attempting to get out of the small, snow-covered lot.

A half hour later, the Santiam Pass caught us off guard with melted snow that had quickly begun to freeze back up in the fading sunlight. It was treacherous and scary, but we made it through. Once we reached the Eugene city limits, I started breathing normally again.

After everything was unpacked and the U-Haul was returned, I didn't drive my car for a month. But I didn't have to.

The city of Eugene has an incredible mass transit system. You absolutely do not need a car to live here in this wonderfully walkable city. There are city bikes available all over town, the EmX (EmeraldXpress) buses are clean-running and plentiful, and the stops are everywhere. These buses also have bike racks attached to the front, and they are almost always in use, so you can bike to the stop, ride the bus, then bike some more! And as I mentioned, the bus stops here really are the bomb.

We also have a lovely train station served by Amtrak, and our airport can now get you to seventeen cities and counting. We are ninety minutes from the Cascades and ninety minutes from the coast. And if you can't head out that far for an adventure, you can always hike Spencer Butte and feel like you are miles away, all within city limits.

The last road trip I took was under incredibly sad circumstances. My younger cousin Dan had died in a truly unfortunate accident, and I was going to San Diego for the memorial service. I could have flown, but the road was calling me. Besides, Dan had always been one to appreciate the drive. *It will be therapeutic*, I thought. And it truly was. Seeing alpenglow on Mt. Shasta moved me to tears. The pink and orange colors mixing with the fading blue sky, a giant snow-capped goddess, earthbound yet touching heaven…

Then, I hit LA, and all those feel-good feelings went right out the window. Traffic, honking, belligerent drivers who just don't care—I ran into all of that. I vowed that, even if it took twice the time, my return route wouldn't be the way I came.

Dan's memorial was as unique and sublime as he was. It was also another glaring reminder to enjoy this life while you can because you never know when it will all be over. After the weekend ended and goodbyes were said, I steered toward the Pacific

Coast Highway, rolled my windows down, and hit the pavement. *It is now time to enjoy the ride.*

My route took me through the adorable seaside towns of Laguna, Newport, Huntington, and Seal Beach. There was a pirate fest going on in Long Beach, and those swashbucklers beckoned me, but I had to keep going. I'll catch you next time, Long Beach! I eventually made it up to Big Sur, got a room for the night, and planned to hike Pfeiffer Big Sur State Park the next morning.

The word "beautiful" doesn't do this part of the country justice. Heavenly, maybe? The hills are filled with brilliantly colored wildflowers, and the sandy paths that cut through lead off to cliffside scenic overlooks that stretch out toward the Pacific. And that's just the beginning. There are the giant redwood forests, which take your breath away and leave you feeling small in the trees' enormous and ageless shadows. I was in awe, perhaps a little high on all the fresh oxygen being produced by these monsters. But the scent of the evergreens mixing with the cool airborne spritz of river water was so soothing, and I sat among the trees and the rocks and the water for a while to take it all in.

I wandered a little more until dusk, not really wanting to leave this magical place but knowing that I had to. I eventually gathered my replenished soul, said goodbye to the forest, and reaffirmed that Western sunsets are indeed the best. Dan would have agreed.

Enjoy the ride.

Chapter 6

THE NEIGHBORHOOD JEDI

Neighbors can be tricky sometimes. You can't choose them. Like most people, I've had nice ones and not-so-nice ones. However, I hit the jackpot when I moved here.

When I lived at the Bailey Apartments, there was a young man who lived in the building across the street from mine. He was there with his parents and his younger brother, the perfect family unit.

Sometimes, I would see him toting groceries inside when his mom returned from the food store, or we would cross paths picking up the mail from the boxes down by the clubhouse. When we did, I couldn't help but notice his ticks. He would mutter certain phrases quietly under his breath and would usually be twisting his hands together or flapping them erratically. He seemed like an ordinary enough twenty-something who was somewhere on the autism spectrum, and I never really paid him much mind other than the occasional neighborly wave, which he would ignore.

But then, on that glorious, warm, spring day, when I opened my windows for the first time, I heard it. It was unmistakable. A sound I knew well. That slightly electric, droning hum of… Could it be? A LIGHTSABER! Then, the words, "I AM A JEDI LIKE MY FATHER BEFORE ME!" rang out across the complex, followed by the crackling whir and pop of the saber as it whacked against the shrubbery.

I feel the need to interject here. Remember, I'm a child of the 1970s. I was almost seven years old when *Star Wars: Episode IV* came out. It's the movie that made me want to be a space princess and kiss Harrison Ford. (For the record, I still want to be a space princess and kiss Harrison.) The film shaped me. Not only did it instill a deep love of science fiction movies that I still hold to this day, but it opened my young mind to the Force, the yin and yang, the energy of the universe, the ebb and flow. It grabbed hold of me more than anything else had at that point in my young life. It was and still is epic. I've never gone to any fan conventions or done the cosplay other than dressing as Leia for Halloween in 1977. But yeah… Huge fan.

Now, back to the lightsaber sounds. When I looked out the window, there he was in all his brown-cloaked glory, a Jedi Knight. He was swinging and spinning with the energy and grace of a classically trained ballet dancer, dueling with an imaginary Darth Vader who would certainly end us all if it weren't for this plucky young rebel, fighting for all that is right.

He reminded me of a simpler time in my life—a time when my imagination would zoom off to that galaxy far, far away, and I was the one flying the Falcon and icing Imperial stormtroopers with my blaster. He was a touchstone.

Throughout the spring and summer, at least once a week, I'd see him pacing the sidewalk in front of his apartment, a warrior at the ready. The robe, the lightsaber, the impeccable reciting of lines—it all was a joy to watch.

I considered going to talk with him on several occasions. I thought if I put on my Leia buns and offered him a candy from my Porg PEZ dispenser, we'd hit it off and have a great afternoon of saving Resistance fighters on the ninth moon of Endor. But

I never did. I didn't want to do anything that might destroy the wholesomeness of his world.

When he and his family moved out, I was sad. I still miss everything about him. Wherever he may be now, I hope he never stops his vigilant watch for any trace of the dark side. And if he does find it, let him strike it down swiftly and justly. He was our neighborhood Jedi, and he kept the Bailey Apartments Sith- and Empire-free from 2016 to 2020.

May the Force be with him always.

Just an aside, in my new 'hood, there is an interesting-looking fellow who wears a long, purple, cloak-type bathrobe when he stands outside his apartment to smoke. His white hair peeks out from beneath his cowl, and I can only think, "Obi-Wan? Could it be? Is that you??" I haven't seen him wielding a lightsaber to date, but he does have a tricked-out walking cane, bedazzled with a multitude of glittery stars and comets and spaceships. He's now my NEW Jedi, a novel cog in the quirky wheel of characters that encompass daily life here, constantly turning.

Chapter 7
COLLEGE

Eugene is a college town, the home to the University of Oregon since 1876. The school mascot was originally the Webfoot, which then changed into the Oregon Duck. Our big, fuzzy drake is affectionately known as Puddles, and he is notably adorable. Sometimes, at the beginning of games, he gets driven into the football stadium on the back of a Harley Davidson motorcycle, which is pretty bad ass.

Some people think ducks are weak animals. They're cute, and they waddle, but have you ever seen an angry duck? If they're serious about it, they can and will hurt you. There are nubs that resemble teeth in the back of that cute yellow bill. Quack, quack, watch your back!

Campus is truly grand in its mix of Second Empire and Gothic Revival style architecture. It's an eclectic blend of buildings that can look ominous as well as inspiring. Home to both the Jordan Schnitzer Museum of Art and the Museum of Natural and Cultural History, the university also serves triple duty as a working arboretum as well as a place of higher learning. The school has always operated on trimesters, which consistently makes me think my girlfriends who work there are discussing being pregnant when they mention their schedules. The men as well now that I think about it.

Sports are a huge part of campus life here. Historic Hayward Field, the track and field stadium, was treated to a major overhaul and recently hosted the 2022 World Athletic Championships. Track fans and athletes alike poured in from around the globe for the competition. It was notably an epic week for both Eugene and for the state of Oregon.

He bites!

U of O mascot Puddles

U of O track stars

The floor of the Matthew Knight Arena, where our basketball team plays, has always mesmerized me. It's somewhat dizzying, very kaleidoscopic, and absolutely unique. All around the perimeter of the court are silhouettes of our state tree, the Douglas fir. Three different shades of yellowy green-gray pine trees overlap each other and grow out toward center court. Kudos to the players who can do what they do and not get vertigo with all that going on.

Aside from the U of O, there are other institutions that call Eugene their home. Bushnell University is a small Christian school that encompasses roughly two downtown city blocks. There's also Lane County Community College whose campus is considerably bigger but somewhat more far removed, located on the outskirts of town. We also have New Hope Christian College, the tiny school on the hill. It sits just up the road from where I used to live. Their seventy-foot, blazing bright cross was illuminated every night, and though I haven't been a churchgoer for some time, it would give me comfort when I'd look at it from my balcony.

Coming to Eugene felt a lot like going off to college again. It was a brand-new chapter in a brand-new city with brand-new friends. Only this time, I felt considerably more comfortable in my own skin. The parallels were there, and over time, while I observed life around campus, I noticed that not much had changed for the younger generations that were here.

There is a fairly active Greek community at the U of O. That means fraternities and sororities. I'll disclose now that I have a love/hate relationship with these organizations. I know that they have their good points, like charity work in the community and the philanthropic events they hold. However, most of the time when I hear about these groups nowadays, it usually involves terrible stories of binge drinking and hazing gone horribly wrong.

Like the stupid white frat boys I saw standing out by a busy intersection near campus, holding a sign that read, "Honk & I'll do a shot." My only thought was if they were black kids, they'd be chased off, if not arrested and taken away in cuffs. This is where everyone should see the white boy privilege.

I didn't always see things as clearly as I do now. Chalk that up to age and a lot of life lessons—serious life lessons. But I do know that teachings come so we can learn things about *ourselves*. It's how our mettle gets tested. It's how we evolve into our best self—by slogging through gut-wrenching trials that show us *who we really are* whether we realize it at the time or not. And college is first and foremost about learning. Not just book smarts but street smarts as well. Sometimes, we think we know exactly what we want to learn in life; other times, the universe intervenes.

My oldest sister was the first to ship off to the University of Maryland when I was barely thirteen. When she returned home for Thanksgiving, she came sporting a sweatshirt with these amazing, emerald-green Greek letters blazing across the front, and I was captivated. My middle sister followed two years later, off to Syracuse when I was a junior in high school. The sweatshirt she came back with was equally cool.

I had seen the movie *Animal House* when I was ten or eleven years old and absolutely loved that film. We all know the story of the scrappy Deltas taking on and defeating both the Omegas *and* Faber College. And if you don't, I encourage you to watch it. It's epic. I knew the lines by heart back then, and I still do.

I had forgotten the film was shot here at the University of Oregon until I came out for my first visit and was reminded. The Omega house as well as Babs and Mandy's red brick colonial with the white columns are still standing. Sadly, Delta house is gone now, replaced by a modern building that serves as office space for Bushnell. Dean Wormer is nowhere in sight.

Looking back, it's easy to see why I always equated college with Greek life. It was what I knew, what I aspired to, and to some extent, what was expected of me. During those years, I thought there could be nothing better. You go to a few parties and get your bid to your favorite house. Then, you get this ready-made group of friends who you go out to fraternity parties and jam like a rock star with and make deep, sisterly bonds for life. Sounds awesome, right?

But I was destined to stay on the periphery of that life. A goddammed independent, or GDI as the sisters and brothers jokingly referred to the non-Greek university kids.

I went through what's known as "rush" my freshman year. I felt I was going in strong. I knew the drill, and I knew what was expected of me. Put on your fashionable clothes, smile, and be pleasant. They'll like you for sure! What could go wrong? As it turned out, an evening Spanish class exam was what tripped me up. That's what.

Ay dios mio! The first quarter exam was on the same night as the Thursday night rush parties, and it counted for a substantial part of our final grade. Go figure the one time I decide to be the good student and *not* blow off this exam, it ends in my collegiate dream being shattered.

The final result: My absence at the parties had left a stain on me. No show meant no sororities extended me invites back. Whether it was fate intervening or just some dumb snafu, I'll never know. All I know is that my heart and soul were banged up good. I was blackballed. Calling me bitter at that particular juncture of my life would have been an understatement.

Many of my friends went on to pledge houses. My roommate Elisabeth and my other bestie Anthony were both Greek, and I knew people in just about every house on campus. I thought for sure I'd get an invitation my sophomore year when I pushed myself to go through the process again at the urging of friends and acquaintances alike.

The universe laughed at that prospect. No such luck. I suppose I just was too much of an outsider. I sure as hell felt like one. It was yet another gentle reminder that the best-laid plans will often go awry.

After I licked my wounds and fixed my spine back into its upright position, I applied to the campus radio station, WWVU-FM, U-92, the Moose. At the time, it was a mere 300-watt powerhouse of twenty-four-hour, student-run programing that had held my interest from the time I'd first considered West Virginia University.

I went into the station interview feeling nervous and sweaty. The usual demons crept into my head and whispered that I was making another mistake, that I wasn't good enough. But within the first five minutes talking with the general manager and station directors, the anxiety slowly faded, and I felt more comfortable. It went well, and one week later, I was hired as a DJ. I finally felt like I'd found my people.

Music had always gotten me through the rough patches growing up. Now, here it was, saving me once again. I had found the island of misfit toys, and they all liked The Cure as much as me! I felt so vindicated, and being a part of this unique group of people turned into one of the best experiences of my life. It was so much better than the other choice. The worst sort of hazing new DJs endured was a 3 a.m. to 6 a.m. air shift, perhaps even a week or two of them. The horror!

Or maybe you'd get pranked. For example, the reggae jock and his pals who were on before me one early morning changed the weather forecast to read, "Warm hummus with a slight chance of baba ganoush." And you bet I said it, word for word. It was maybe my third or fourth night on the air, so the training wheels were still on when that happened. Damn you, Rasta Jon! You got me with your funny food-related weathercast.

I used to think about how my life might have been different had I stayed on the path I thought was right for me, the path that my family had inadvertently paved. Would I be the same person I am today? I've always taken the road less traveled; it just took this experience to make me see and truly embrace it. The most valuable lesson learned through college: When the door won't open for you, *stop pushing on it.*

I drove for a rideshare service for a year or so here in Eugene, and during that time, I had many sorority and fraternity kids in my back seat. They weren't all that different from the brothers and sisters I knew while I was in school. Just younger and following the fashion of the day. And when they were in my car, they were usually intoxicated.

A case in point moment was when I picked up a group heading to their winter formal. All prettied up and smelling of pre-game drinks and perfume, they spoke about new pledges and other sisters with venom on their tongues. "She's not Kappa material." The boys were just as bad.

A few weeks later, while out driving, I passed a homeless guy wearing an Alpha Phi sweatshirt—like the actual Greek letters, not just some pledge or homecoming T-shirt. He looked disheveled and high and dirty, and he didn't have shoes on his feet. I'm sure the sisters would not be happy with that. He's not Alpha material.

Chapter 8

BOOZE & DRUGS

People love their substances. You can't convince me otherwise. And everyone has some sort of addiction, be it caffeine, nicotine, alcohol, marijuana, cocaine, adrenaline…

Altered states of consciousness are interesting things. We lose our inhibitions and get a little nutty, and it feels good, so why not? I found a bumper sticker years ago that read "In Search of the Eternal Buzz." It spoke to me: *Fuck if that isn't true!* And fuck if this serotonin-lacking chick will ever stop looking for that buzz.

In Eugene, you can search around and find new places to intoxicate yourself for weeks on end. We've got breweries, wineries, and dispensaries for miles. Go searching in the cow pastures, and you may just find some psilocybin mushrooms if you look hard enough.

In a few months, you won't even have to do that because Oregon recently voted "yes" on legalization of them for medicinal purposes. Hard drugs have also been decriminalized here. Class one narcotics possession in small amounts for personal use will no longer have jail time as a punishment. It's still in the early stages but shows every sign of working better than the former model. Baby steps.

But booze is still the drug of choice for many in this town—for many in a lot of towns. God bless America, we do love our drinks.

Day drinking is normalized on TV shows, in advertising, pretty much everywhere now.

Years ago, I remember visiting with my sister, and she had the *Today* show on as we were having breakfast and getting ready to go out. Along with news, entertainment, and cooking segments, it was also "Fishbowl Friday." That meant Kathy Lee and Hoda were drinking what looked like a very nice Cabernet during the newscast. They giggled and made mistakes, and I supposed this was some producer's attempt at making them seem a little more relatable. This was my first experience seeing this concept of morning cocktails on a news-type show, and I just thought it made them look…well, drunk.

About a year later, I saw *The Kelly Clarkson Show* had a segment called "Wine to Mommy" where unhappy mothers got on their webcams, complained about things, and drank. Hey, it's 5 p.m. somewhere, right?

I also recall some other national news show unveiling a recipe for The Quarantini. It was a potent little cocktail that was partially Prosecco. According to the newscaster, the bubbles make it an acceptable morning beverage!

And while on the topic of bubbles, how can anyone forget the epic drunk duo that dominated New Year's Eve viewing: Anderson and Andy. What a sweet couple of drunks!

You can get beer, cider, or wine at any of the local movie theaters here in Eugene. And I'd have never expected to see a bar in my local grocery store. It's not a fully stocked one with hard liquor, but the Fred Meyer on the west side of town has seven taps of the best local beer and hard cider, so you can grab a pint of either and take a break from your shopping. This is a prime example of how we are a society that worships the bottle, then are numb or judgmental when alcoholism eventually rears its ugly head.

I'm going to get dark here. I should hate drugs and alcohol. I should despise them both based on the fact that I've lost too many dear friends to addictions. Fuck knows how many friends and family members I've watched "overdo it" only to witness repeat performances again and again. Those who were out of control and in denial, I've cut ties with. It hurts too much to hang on and watch the mayhem. The demons won't let them see that we are all responsible for our own intake, and if things get out of hand, it's time to stop. It blinds them to getting help and support. Unfortunately, it is a daily battle that is lost more often than won.

I've had three wingmen in my life, and I've mourned three deaths.

I met Anthony freshman year in college. We were the best of friends for years until a bad reaction to seizure medicine killed him. Reaction to what, I will never know. Anthony was always a partier who truly loved the altered state. My mom called him a vagabond on more than one occasion and was probably a little scared that her daughter could take off to Mexico with this character, strictly on a whim. He was a writer, a poet, and the one who introduced me to what is affectionately known in the stoner world as the Wake 'n Bake. That's when you roll a fat joint and get high first thing in the morning. Mixed with some strong coffee and good music, I did and still do enjoy it. Think of it as the weed smoker's equivalent of a bloody Mary or mimosa. The breakfast of champions!

Heroin/fentanyl took David, my brother from another mother. We met in second grade and lived in the same neighborhood. Growing up together, David and I shared a love of music and a hatred for school. We both slacked at the same level. Imagine my surprise when I sadly walked in to the first day of summer school, feeling like some dumb loser, only to see David sitting there in the back row of desks. "*Holy shit, you failed Biology too*?!" We were close even through years of not seeing each other. I know he and his family tried hard for a sober David. I saw the hospital bills and the anguish he faced. He told me about his rehabs and sponsors and all his demons before he left. I'm heartbroken that those demons won.

Alcohol took Jeff. He was one of my romantic interests whom I met when I was twenty-one. We met at a bar off campus that was having a "Drinkin' with Lincoln" night. Five bucks at the door meant all the crap beer you could drink. We were lovers, then friends, then lovers again, then friends. These were the college years.

We lost touch after graduation but reconnected in 2010. When I saw him after all that time had passed, all I wanted to do was to help him, this man whom I'd loved. I spent time with Jeff in the throes of his alcoholism, and it was nothing short of devastating. The mixed moods, the blacking out, the utterly selfish behavior—it was painful.

One night, as I cradled him in my arms, trying to reassure him that he could get help and be better, he looked at me with tear-filled eyes and whispered, "Please kill me." At that moment, I felt every ounce of pain, fear, anger, and shame that has ever run through an addict's body. It shot through me like lightning, charring my heart. The fun drunk had left. A long time ago, he'd left. All that remained now was this broken man, begging for me to end his nightmare. I never found out his cause of death. A link to his sparse obituary was all that came to me. I didn't need a coroner's report. He died of alcoholism.

So, here I am now in a town that has always had a reputation for being a haven for illegal substances since before time itself. No wonder John Belushi loved this place! The stocky yet agile actor was known to visit often. The story is that he'd get all tanked up, then perform with friends down in the lounge of the Eugene Hotel. The idea for The Blues Brothers was born there. It seems like Bluto just never wanted the party to end. Well, we all know how it finally ended for him.

Now, the bars and wineries are back open after a yearlong COVID shutdown, and my marijuana dispensary has come raging back with a very nice loyalty program. Sin tax is nothing new. Full legalization of marijuana has been gaining traction across the country for the simple reason that the money pays for things like schools and roads and a million other social services that are sorely needed. People don't necessarily like paying their taxes every April 15th, but they sure as hell don't mind kicking in a few extra dollars at the register as long as they can get fucked up!

And this willingness to pay is now becoming evident; 2021 saw the marijuana tax generating more tax dollars than the alcohol tax in Illinois. The sweet leaf beat the bottle in the Land of Lincoln! Perhaps this is a sign that a new substance is poised to take over the American landscape. If yes, I'll happily toke to that!

Chapter 9

THE COUNTRY FAIR

Within the first month of living in Eugene, I had at least five different people ask me if I planned on going to the Oregon Country Fair. I figured it was just another fair, rife with corn dog stands, rigged games of chance, and sketchy carnival rides. No. That is not, nor has it ever been, the case with this fair. As it was told, this one is in a class all its own. Something to be experienced, not just talked about. It doesn't take place in Eugene proper, but it's a mere fifteen-minute drive west of town, and I certainly can't write a book about this town without including it.

Veneta is our sister city to the west, and every second weekend in July, this small neighboring burg hosts a three-day party of sorts. It's a weekend full of arts and music and food and fairies and freaks of all shapes and sizes. People come from all points to take part in the magic. And it really is magic. This fair embraces the surreal and fantastic with a warm, mossy hug.

The Oregon Country Fair is held on roughly ten acres of property that sits on the banks of the Long Tom River. Winding wooded paths lead to open, airy meadows. Once the fair opens, vendor stands line these paths, and art installations grow in the meadows. Performance stages of various sizes pepper the woods and are home to musicians, comedians, dancers, poets, jugglers, magicians, puppeteers, and actors of all kinds. Take in a vaudeville show, then buy some homespun crafts. There are alternative energy vendors, along with yurt and tiny house sellers. So much sustainability makes one hopeful.

Peace

The fair property also includes archaeological sites protected by state law. It is thought to have previously been a gathering place for the Kalapuya tribe of Native Americans. No wonder the whimsy still lives in these woods, unjaded and laughing. You can feel the energy as you immerse yourself in the greenery.

The first time I went to the Oregon Country Fair, we were met in the parking lot by an elf riding a unicorn. The elf was a teenage girl, and her steed was a white saddle horse with a rainbow horn protruding from his forehead. This was going to be fun! At the main entrance stood a thirty-foot-tall metal dragon head, and inside the gaping mouth was the information and will call booth.

The mystical fan dancer

Piano in the woods

Parts

These cavemen couldn't keep up!

Near the main entrance are numerous signs that read the event is billed as "family friendly," so there is no sale of alcohol. The same signs state you may see naked people. One thing is guaranteed: You will see a lot, and I mean A LOT, of painted titties! And butts too, as there are *many* thong-wearing fairgoers letting it all hang out. And some thongs have tails! Fox, horse, and rabbit are always popular.

All bags are inspected upon entry for adult beverages and weed, but that doesn't stop the fair folk from ingesting all sorts of mind-altering substances ahead of time (please see previous chapter: Booze & Drugs). That, and marijuana is very easy to hide! Clouds of pine-scented smoke drift through the compound, floating out from the alcoves and treehouses where joints are passed in semi-secrecy. As long as you keep it cool, no one is going to hassle you. That's not the fair way!

Fairgoers get crazy with headpieces from simple flower rings to elaborate millinery and costumes from basic to wow. Marching brass bands, some twenty musicians strong, belt out Journey and Nat King Cole songs as they parade through the woods. It's like Mardi Gras, the Easter Parade, and Christmas all rolled into one!

The six-foot-tall robin egg in a giant nest, the five cavemen passed out under a giant sun sphere sculpture, and the fan dancer I had a moment with are locked in my memory forever. There was also an old, out-of-tune grand piano someone put under a hundred-year-old maple. A guy who resembled Tom Waits was playing it while his audience lounged on the Persian rugs scattered around. Moroccan lanterns and origami birds hung from the branches, along with spinning mobiles that featured cut up x-rays of someone's injured arm and leg. They floated in the sunshine like strange kites, beckoning you to look closer. All weirdness is welcomed. It doesn't ever have to make sense.

My second time at the fair, I was introduced to Jai Ho, and there under a giant circus tent, I found *the* true happy dance. This fun boogie takes Bollywood beats and traditional Indian dance moves and blends it with stomping feet and hands waving to the heavens. And oh, Holy Vishnu, it is FUN! The act of dancing with a hundred people in synchronicity is thoroughly energizing, much like group prayer or group singing. It's a collective boosting of energy and vibrations, and it absolutely resonates. It's also one hell of a workout! HIGHLY RECOMMENDED!

2019 was the fifty-year anniversary of the fair, and though it's changed from the time of its inception when peace, love, and nude hippies were in their prime, it still rolls the way its creators would have wanted. The spirit is absolutely there. It is an eco-friendly, zero-waste, fully volunteer, no-alcohol event. To be fair, some people gripe about that last one. Drinkers don't like dry events and get a little miffed when they can't imbibe.

The third fair I attended was unexpectedly hot and dusty. Pacific Northwest summers are usually mild, but not that year. Even in the shade, the heat was oppressive at ninety-five degrees.

My friend Zac had mercifully found us a small patch of shade, and while he was laying down his beach towel to sit on, one particularly crabby woman yelled out to him, "You don't own this land, white man!" *Well… neither do you, sunshine, but here we are.*

We didn't know if her comment was made as a reminder or as a dig. Maybe it was a combination of both. Perhaps she wanted her personal space and this was her way of getting it. She'll be as obnoxious as possible so no one will want to sit next to such a pill.

I thought she needed to chill in the Flow Zone! That's the tent to go to if you want to hula hoop or play with devil sticks or learn how to juggle or get your hacky sack game on point. Push out the jive, bring in the love!

All in all, the Oregon Country Fair is an institution, one that should be visited and experienced at least once. I hope it never goes away. Whether you're sober or intoxicated, I assure you the time spent in the trees is something you won't soon forget—nor would we ever want you to.

Chapter 10

DATING

Dating is a shit show all over the place, not just in Eugene. But with this place being the unique enclave that it is, I guarantee there are going to be highly interesting people swimming in the dating pool.

I've been on both sides of the partnership spectrum, so I feel I've had a generous helping of each. I was joyously attached for fourteen out of seventeen years and know what it's like to live in that dynamic. It has its pros and cons, as does being single. I've been happily unattached for quite some time now, but I'm still a human. I mean, who doesn't get the itch for sexy time on occasion? A girl can't live on vibrators and fantasy forever. Or can she? We are all familiar with that old adage about finding the prince—that, in order to do it, one must kiss many frogs. Well, some of those frogs are what make me think I can be happily unattached for all eternity!

Now, meeting a potential love online has never appealed to me. I find it odd. I'm old school and like to have things happen organically without text messages being involved. But, when in Rome, so up went the stats. "Hi, I'm Dee. I'm a great independent chick with a penchant for bad boys who have daddy issues. Do you have what I'm looking for?" That seemed honest enough, and it really was what I was thinking when trying to piece together an intriguing and smart paragraph or two, but I didn't write that. It's hard enough doing this without actually inviting the deranged to hit you up.

I once had a friend describe dating after the age of thirty. "It's like trying to show someone that you are, in fact, the shiniest, least damaged thing at the dump." Fuck if that's not the truest thing ever! And at middle age, everyone has damage. Life does that to us—I get it. But sometimes, there is a little TOO much damage. This person doesn't shine. Noticing it early on will save you both time and lipstick.

Let's start with The Profile. Transparency is welcomed; however, there is such a thing as too much information. It goes along with too much damage! One of the funnier profiles I saw was some guy whose tagline was "Hep C positive and been to prison five times." I appreciated the candid nature of this fellow, but swipe left.

I've noticed that the younger generations love their facial piercings and their face tattoos. I've always been an advocate for self-expression, but I find that sort of body modification so unattractive. It's just not my thing. Regardless, the dating apps are full of these types. For instance, RamRod69 had a face full of jangly hoops and badly done tattooed script over both eyebrows. Whoever inked those words could have used the calligraphy scroll from the tiny art gallery for better reference. Swipe left. Someone else can date Post Malone; it's not going to be me.

"Becoming his baby" said he prefers to be dominant and that he wants to see you in diapers. I never thought so many different kinks were possible until I ventured into this world. I now firmly believe everybody has some sort of fetish. Vanilla sex just won't cut it anymore. Perhaps I'm outdated, but I see vanilla as a perfect base. It's delicious! You can add things to it and make it spectacular. A few cherries, some chocolate sauce, a banana… Toppings! But the basics and those who like them keep eluding me.

Tomtongue's pic was just roast beef slabs laying on a baking tray. That's it. No other pics, no profile, nothing. Again, it's crude as fuck, but at least he's direct. The man wants to dwell in the house of meat curtains, aka vagina. Got it! Probably married and looking for a side chick. There are a lot of those. Swipe left.

Then, there was the guy in the fuzzy silver unicorn outfit, who stated he loves a good dark roast coffee and well-crafted beer along with his costume fetish. Don't bother responding if you drink Folgers or Bud Light.

Tlapaltehuilotl (which means "amethyst" in Aztec) had a profile that caught my attention. Keep in mind, one thing endemic to Oregon online dating is fish pictures. There are a tremendous number of pics with guys holding up fish they caught. It's an outdoorsy state, so there are always excessive trout photos. Well, this guy's profile was trout laden and started off in the most normal of ways. "I like camping, hiking, fishing, and submissive females who know their place." Well, okay then. I can only think Tlapaltehuilotl would be expecting me to clean that fish and cook it for him, among other things. Swipe left.

Finding the person whose damage syncs up with yours really is the trick, online and off. Do your demons play well together? Ask yourself that before thinking, *Let's see if we can give this a try.*

Jed caught my attention by messaging that he loves the fire of red hair. That's more words than some of these people can manage. "Ur hot." "S'up." Those seem to be standard icebreakers in the online dating world, so his opening line stood out. *Let's see if we can give this a try.* We exchanged numbers, and I heard from him via text the next day. He opened with, "If I told you what the tree of life is and that I know how to fix almost everything wrong with the world today, would you believe me and want to help me make it so?" Wow. I gotta see where this is going to go… And oh, it went, honey!

He was a cannabis enthusiast and grower, so that had me intrigued. Now was the time in the conversation to ask what he did for work. This is always dangerous territory. What I got for a response was impressive in both length and bravado.

"I hate to tell you, but I was disabled in 2001 at work. I've healed quite a lot since then. I have been a grower, probably one of the top ten in the country, but I haven't been able to grow now for several years. After getting divorced, my SS and disability is not quite enough to pay for a place to do it."

He's bringing so much to the table! He continued on about how renting grow space has been ruined by renters, and now he can't do what he's best at. So, now he works odd jobs, donates plasma, digs through recycling for scrap, and wants to find someone to help get his tree of life started.

So yeah, the tree…what I was *really* curious about. Apparently, it's a giant cannabis plant that can give us everything. It can replace every product on the planet. It'll be able to provide clothing, housing, food, energy. It will replace money! *Oh sweetie, don't I wish!*

It was when he began the rant on big pharma that I decided to bow out of this conversation. But then: "Psychedelics can replace antidepressants." *Yes, true! Hmmm, not so fast there, D… Maybe I can score some mushrooms off this guy!*

Living in America, I know that big pharma sucks. However, if you take my Cymbalta and Xanax away from me, you just might lose a limb. I come from a very long line of depressed eastern

Europeans, and I rely on those meds and marijuana to keep me sane. I've been off them and on them and off them… The off is not pretty. It's why "better living through chemistry" is sort of my mantra now.

Jed's tirade continued, with him telling me how he has a friend in LA who is a true healer and is on board with the tree. This friend used to be a doctor but now is living a life underground. Apparently, if the wrong people hear where the former doctor is, they'll make him disappear. *Hmmm, truth is always stranger than fiction.* By then, I'd really had my fill of this guy. I politely told him that I didn't think I was the right person for his tree and said goodbye. Back to the pond with you, strange little frog.

Another highlight was Rob. He was cute! A little hairy for my taste but tall and burly with soft eyes, so he had my attention. He said he works at one of the breweries here in town and likes to hike. *Let's see if we can give this a try.* No kids—bonus! I like kids, don't get me wrong. I just like to give them back. I'm not a mom. I'm an aunt four times over, and my nephews are very dear to me. But being around little ones and even big ones on the regular? Nah…not my thing.

So, a coffee date got scheduled for a Saturday at one of the many local java joints in town. I prettied myself up and headed out, slightly anxious as usual, but the Xanax was helping. As soon as I found parking, my text pinged, and it was him.

"Hey, I know this is short notice, but I have to cancel."

Okay, it happens. Not the first time. Won't be the last.

"My daughter was just admitted to the BHU at Riverbend."

Holy fuck. His profile said he didn't have kids… This is a nice development. I suppose he thought teenagers aren't children. I absolutely am aware that dating profiles are full of half-truths, bravado, and lies. But sweetheart, I've got my own BHU problems going on in my head. I don't need any more.

And how can I ever forget Larry. He was another normal-on-the-surface guy, and I truly was interested in getting to know him better. I thought it was a bit weird when he asked how long my nails were. *So, maybe he likes well-kept hands. Some people like feet. Perhaps, with him, it's hands.* Turns out that Lar likes his nipples pinched. Hard. He wanted me to draw blood. Thanks for playing, but no.

Last but certainly not least, there was Greg. We talked for a few days, and he told me that he has two teenaged kids, both a son and a daughter. Teenagers aren't a problem, right? As we were on our way out to get drinks and dinner, his phone rang. It was his fifteen-year-old daughter who had just gotten caught shoplifting underwear at JCPenney and needed to be bailed out of the store jail. So, we went and did just that. Best date ever.

I firmly believe I was born under a bad sign for dating. I have always had the vibe that attracts the broken. And there is a metric fuck ton of broken out there. But we all still have to make the effort and do the dance if we want romantic companionship, and it truly shouldn't be that hard. Just answer the following questions for me: Do you work? Does your dick work? Do you have any raging drug or alcohol problems? God help me, please, are you stable??

I've gotten both laughs and serious insight in regard to human behavior over my years of dating. The pics run the gamut from fellas who look like hardcore serial killers to the ones holding their little purse-sized dogs. Then, there are the guys who *look* like their little purse-sized dogs. I know sometimes people choose pets based on what they find attractive, but damn. I never realized how many dudes resemble French bulldogs in this town.

And just how many of these guys are named Brendan/Brandon/Dustin/Justin anyway? Their profiles run together with bland sameness akin to a Pottery Barn catalog. "I love to laugh, romantic dinners, walks on the beach." Well, who doesn't, Junior? Give me a little more substance, please. Not the same boring generic lines we've all come to accept as small talk. It's cookie cutter conversation at its finest, and it bores me to tears.

Then, there's always the "My kid comes first" guy. He wants you to know that you'll come second, if at all, right off the bat. My response to this is always the same: *No shit. Just ask the BHU guy*! Your kid is always going to come first. It's called being a parent.

After a year of failed dates, I stopped. I canceled my dating subscription and told myself to take a break. There is freedom in being single, and I needed to embrace that notion and live it. So, I did. For three years, I entered into a state of Zen-like focus on myself and worked on healing the parts of me that needed it.

Looking at your darkest moments and finally making friends with and accepting them is a challenge. It's the shadow work we all are better for doing, despite the discomfort. It allows us to grow and change, and that is one of the healthiest things to do for yourself.

But you know what else is healthy? SEX. And they said it wouldn't just show up at the door. But then it did! It happened up at a client's place in the south hills. It was only going to be a quick visit, and I wasn't expecting to be seeing anyone, so I went out "unkempt." No makeup, hair in a do-rag, braless. I may as well have been wearing a housecoat and curlers.

I was wrapping things up with my work when I heard a forceful knock at the door. I opened it only to find two Lane County line workers, hunky as the day is long, standing there like a couple of

Greek gods. OH DEAR, SWEET BABY JESUS! These two were beautiful. And I was NOT at that moment. Let me tell you, there's *nothing* that makes a woman feel uglier than being in the presence of good-looking people when she resembles a bog witch.

One Adonis told me they needed to cut some trees on the property and had to have the homeowner sign off, etc. Looking at them both, all I could feel was that tingly spark that makes us remember the fun, the joy, of being alive.

Before you think anything raunchy, I told them they needed to come back later in the afternoon and sent them on their way. No Penthouse Forum stories for you! But as I watched their adorable butts walk down the driveway, I realized it was time to clean up my appearance and get back on the dating merry-go-round for another spin.

So, now, I'm talking with Oliver. He's different from the others in that he actually speaks! Clearly in sentences even. Many of them just send the utterances I mentioned along with their dick pic, so he's already got an overwhelming edge.

Throughout all my dating mishaps, or perhaps in spite of them all, here I am again, the eternal optimist. Always willing to put myself out there for another letdown, but I'm not feeling that with him so far. *Let's see if we can give this a try.*

Chapter 11
SPRINGFIELD

Across the Willamette River to the east lies Eugene's sister city of Springfield. It's roughly half the size of Eugene and about as quaint, and the rents are slightly lower. Two things Springfield holds highly dear are its native son and author Ken Kesey and long-running TV show *The Simpsons*. Matt Groening, one of the show's creators, is a Portland native. He picked heavily from his surroundings when it came to developing character names and, of course, the name of his fictional town.

There is no Springfield Gorge to speak of there, nor is there Mr. Burns's power plant. But there are a handful of lumber and pulp mills whose steam towers could possibly be seen as nuclear. Those things also release some highly stinky smells thanks to all that pulp production. It's why the rents are cheaper there. Sometimes, you have to close up your windows to avoid it.

Mt. Pisgah is an easy double for Mt. Springfield, and Main Street is, well…Main Street. For a while, Moe's Tavern existed, but it's gone now, replaced by a less dank establishment whose bar stools aren't covered in duct tape. I'm sure there is probably a tire fire burning somewhere in town on any given day, but not continually.

PublicHouse on A Street could maybe pass for Reverend Lovejoy's church. This former house of worship was transformed into a beer garden, whiskey bar, and food truck court. You can still feel the spiritual energy emanating through the stained-glass windows when you're sharing libations. It's like drinking with God! When spring comes, the outdoor patio area is covered in purple wisteria blooms, making a lovely setting for a date or special occasion. It's one of my favorite places.

But the best thing about Springfield is the murals. So many Simpsons murals… I'm going to let the photos speak for me now. Enjoy!

By Nick Simpson

By Nick Simpson

By Nick Simpson

By Nick Simpson

By Nick Simpson

By Nick Simpson

By Nick Simpson

By Nick Simpson

By Nick Simpson

By Nick Simpson

Old School

By Nick Simpson

By Nick Simpson

By Diane Johnson –
The Simpsons

By Nick Simpson

Chapter 12

GOODNIGHT BUT NOT GOODBYE

These stories are excerpts from my life: the book of Dee. And this book is my love letter to a city—a city that grabbed and sculpted me into a person I knew I could and wanted to be: authentic, compassionate, strong, smart, resilient, and real. There were times when this place lost its shine, but only for a minute.

Not everyone sees Eugene as I do. To most people, this place is just a blip on a map. But this town has given me insight and lessons that won't soon be forgotten. The west side is industrial and gritty. It taught me to stay humble. The north end is bohemian. It taught me to be true to myself. The south hills are posh. They taught me to strive for more. And the east side is collegiate. It taught me to never stop learning.

I don't necessarily believe in fate, but I do believe there are signs and signals and guides all around us to help aid in this journey of life. We just need to see them, to feel them, to acknowledge them and then follow them.

I had been in Eugene for two years when I hit a horrible mental rough patch. Doubting myself and fearful of what could become of me, I went to get some sunshine at the community pool. My friend Randi and I were lying on our chaise loungers when I had a visit from a little angel.

The fairy sprite named Faith found me there on a hot day that felt anything but summery to me. We watched as she played with her older brothers, jumping in and out of the water like an acrobatic sea lion pup. I smiled while watching her spin and twirl, and she eventually noticed my grin. Fixing her gaze on me intently, she then yelled, "I can't see your eyes!" and came skipping over. As I peered over my dark sunglasses, I looked at her bright baby blues and felt her lean in to press her forehead against mine. It felt like the whole moment lasted hours, although I know it was mere seconds. But when she stared back into my eyes, giggled, then said, "Love," I knew things would be alright.

I know I'll never leave this place. It's just too magical. This is a city with heavy rain but even more rainbows. And the sun shines through the precipitation here! Those drops shimmer like diamonds, prisms caught in the atmosphere.

Eugene is a constant reminder to take time, embrace your life, and do what makes you happy. It tells everyone if you want to succeed, do what you *like* in life, not what you feel you *should* do. Success can be measured in many different ways, and Eugene showcases that fact every single day. It's a place that *wants* you to follow your dream, to *not* be afraid to fail.

Be like Eugene and keep evolving. Be aware that education and the arts slay stagnation. Be like Eugene and have empathy. Life is cyclical, and we all need help at times. Be like Eugene and spend time in nature. Know that, without all of it, we'd be lost. Be like Eugene and smell the roses. They are everywhere in this town and everywhere in the world. Go look for them, find them, and breathe the beauty in deep.

Be like Eugene.

Welcome Eugene

LILA

LIVE THE DREAM

LOVE IS A CHOICE.

ABOUT THE AUTHOR

D.E. Novak lives blissfully in Eugene, Oregon, with her beloved cats and betta fishes. She is a graduate of West Virginia University as well as the school of life. An avid figure skater, she also skis, hikes, and loves to garden. You are going to want her on your team in trivia games, especially when the categories are music or movies. And she's been known to rock the karaoke mic with gusto! Lastly, if you ask her nicely, she'll even read your tarot cards.